Vietnam

Karen O'Connor

Carolrhoda Books, Inc. / Minneapolis

Photo Acknowledgments

Photos, maps, and artworks are used courtesy of John Erste, pp. 1, 2–3, 7, 16–17, 21, 31, 33, 38–39; Laura Westlund, pp. 4, 24–25, 43; © TRIP/J. Sweeney, pp. 6 (left), 16, 35 (top); Rick and Susie Graetz, pp. 6 (right), 7, 14, 18 (both), 22, 22–23, 26 (bottom), 28, 30; © Nevada Wier, pp. 8, 10 (bottom), 11 (bottom), 12 (top), 15 (both), 17 (left), 25 (both), 29, 31, 32 (both), 33, 36, 37 (both), 40, 44; © TRIP/N. Kealey, p. 9 (left); © TRIP/R. Squires, p. 9 (right); © TRIP/H. Bower, pp. 10 (top), 35 (bottom); © John Elk III, pp. 11 (top), 13, 17 (right), 19, 27, 41 (bottom); © TRIP/A. Tovy, p. 12 (bottom); © Brian A. Vikander, p. 20 (left); © TRIP/A. Ghazzal, pp. 20 (right), 26 (top); © Sophie Dauwe/Robert Fried Photography, pp. 23, 41 (top); © TRIP/R. Nichols, p. 24; © TRIP/B.Vikander, pp. 34, 42. Cover photo of Vietnamese girls by © TRIP/R. Nichols.

Carolrhoda Books, Inc.
A Division of the Lerner Publishing Group
241 First Avenue North
Minneapolis, Minnesota 55401 U.S.A.

Website address: www.lernerbooks.com

Library of Congress Cataloging-in-Publication Data

O'Connor, Karen, 1938–
  Vietnam / by Karen O'Connor.
    p. cm. — (Ticket to)
  Includes index.
  Summary: Briefly describes the people, geography, government, religion, language, customs, and lifestyles of modern-day Vietnam.
    ISBN 1–57505–142–7 (lib. bdg. : alk. paper)
    1. Vietnam—Juvenile Literature. [1. Vietnam.] I. Title.
  II. Series
  DS556.3.016   1999b
  959.7—dc21   98–52660

Manufactured in the United States of America
1 2 3 4 5 6 – JR – 04 03 02 01 00 99

Contents

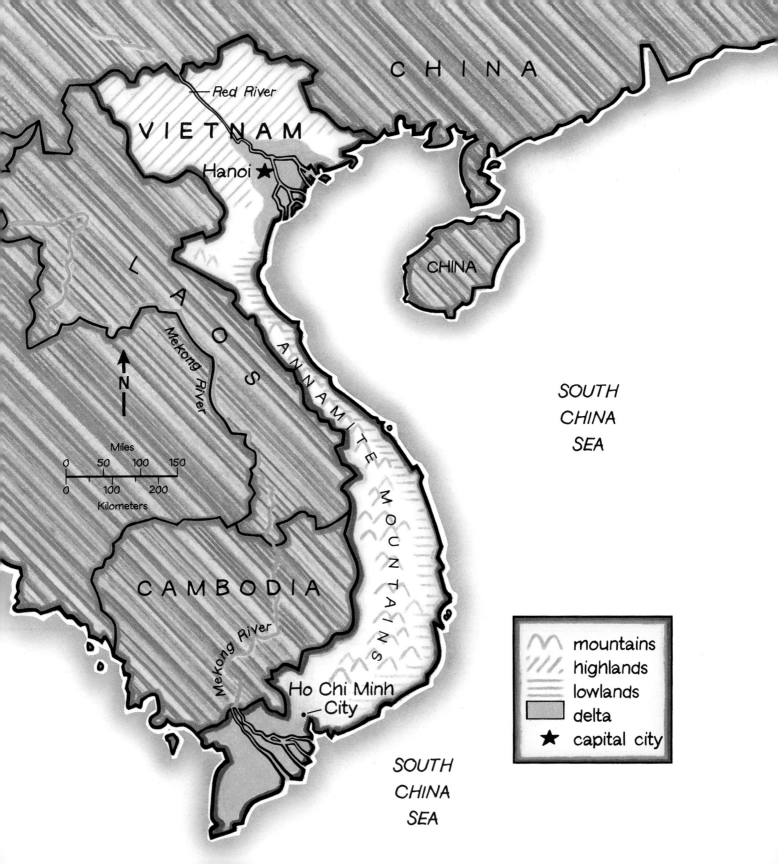

CHINA

Red River

VIETNAM

Hanoi ★

CHINA

L A O S

Mekong River

ANNAMITE MOUNTAINS

SOUTH
CHINA
SEA

N

Miles
0   50   100   150
0   100   200
Kilometers

CAMBODIA

Mekong River

Ho Chi Minh
City

SOUTH
CHINA
SEA

〽️ mountains
▨ highlands
≡ lowlands
▧ delta
★ capital city

Welcome!

Vietnam is a long, thin country. Does its shape remind you of the letter S? Vietnam lies in Asia, the world's biggest **continent.** The South China Sea laps at eastern and southern Vietnam.

Map Whiz Quiz

Take a look at the **map** on page four. Trace the outline of Vietnam onto a piece of paper. Can you spot the Mekong River? Color that blue. What about the Red River? Use red for that. Find China and mark that with an "N" for north. Color the river **deltas** green.

Vietnam has three neighbors. Separated from Vietnam by the Annamite **Mountain Range,** Laos and Cambodia lie to the west. China is Vietnam's neighbor to the north.

Rice grows well in Vietnam's lush, wet fields.

Rivers

Most people in Vietnam live near the Red River in the north or the Mekong River in the south. The rivers travel across Vietnam to the oceans. **Canals** cross the countryside. They bring water from the rivers to farms.

Huge winds called **monsoons** bring tons of rain to Vietnam. Wild storms called **typhoons** swirl in

Grab a coat! Rainstorms come often in Vietnam.

Why the Monsoon Comes Every Year

The princess My Nuong wanted to marry. Spirit of the Sea and Spirit of the Mountain wanted to be her husband. Both set out to bring her gifts, and the princess decided to marry the first one to arrive. When Spirit of the Mountain arrived first with jewels and fruits, the princess married him. Spirit of the Sea was very jealous. Every summer, he tries to win the princess by sending monsoons to the mountain where the princess and her husband live.

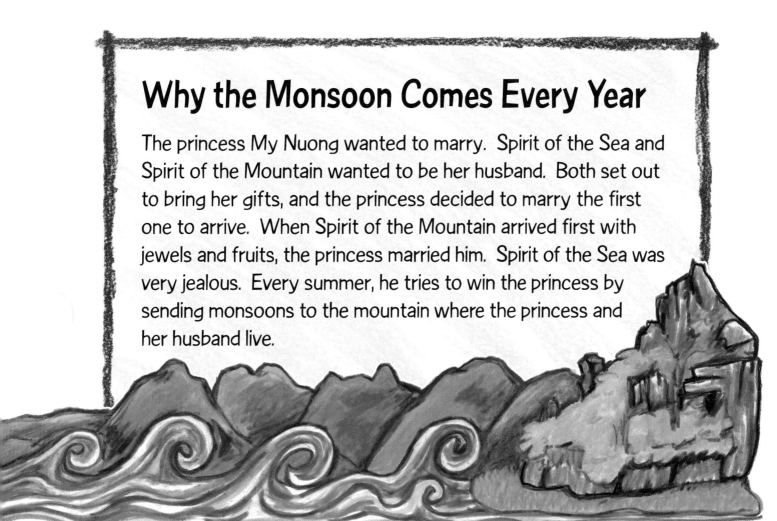

from the ocean with giant waves and powerful winds.

Boats line the shores of the Red River.

People use bamboo from Vietnam's rain forests to make furniture, tools, and more.

Forests

Green! That is the color of Vietnam. Green fields spread near the rivers. **Tropical rain forests** cover the mountains. Leafy jungles coat parts of southern Vietnam. Clumps of trees sprout near the coasts and rivers.

Slithery snakes, playful monkeys, and thundering elephants all call Vietnam's forests home.

Clever farmers carve fields into the sides of mountains (above). *Trees thrive on the country's wet, marshy shores* (left).

People

Most people living in Vietnam are **ethnic Vietnamese.** A long time ago, a group of people from China settled along the Red River. Some of the Chinese newcomers married members of other **ethnic groups** who lived nearby.

These ethnic Vietnamese kids laugh it up.

The old kingdom of Champa lies near the Mekong Delta. Modern-day relatives of Champa's early residents (called the Cham) live in nearby villages.

That created the Vietnamese ethnic group. Most ethnic Vietnamese have black hair and brown eyes.

Montagnards

In French the word *montagnard* means "highlander." Some of Vietnam's ethnic groups, such as the Red Zao *(right)*, like life in Vietnam's Mountains. So they are often known as Montagnards.

Crowded House

A young girl lends a hand.

How many brothers and sisters do you have? In Vietnam a kid might answer, "Lots!" Most families have four or five kids, but some have more. Kids and parents usually share their home with grandparents, aunts, uncles, and cousins. It can get crowded!

Family members pose with the bride and groom. Weddings are special events!

All in the Family

Here are the Vietnamese names for family members.

grandfather	*ong*	(OONG)
grandmother	*ba*	(BAH)
father	*cha*	(CHAH)
mother	*ma*	(MAH)
uncle	*bac*	(BAHK)
aunt	*co*	(COH)
son	*con tai*	(cahn TYE)
daughter	*con gai*	(cahn GYE)
older brother	*ahn*	(AHN)
younger brother	*trai*	(TRY)
older sister	*chi*	(CHIH)
younger sister	*gai*	(GY)

So everyone tries to cooperate. Kids are supposed to respect and obey their parents. Older people are considered very wise.

Big Cities

Ho Chi Minh City is Vietnam's biggest city. The busy

Street Shopping

Farmers sell fresh vegetables and fruit at open-air markets. Crafts are popular buys, too. Shoppers **bargain** with sellers, hoping for a good price. Street stalls sell yummy treats such as fried bananas.

streets are crowded! Walkers watch out for motorbikes, bicycles, and *cyclos.* City kids spend their days at school. Adults go to work. At sidewalk cafés, folks chat and play cards.

People and cars jam this Vietnamese street (left). *Why not hitch a ride on a cyclo* (above)?

Country Life

Most Vietnamese farmers grow rice on their wide, wet **rice paddies.** Gardens are full of vegetables and fruit. Other fields have crops

A water buffalo cools off in a river after a hard day's work.

such as soybeans and cotton.

Farming is a lot of work! Sturdy water buffalo pull plows and carts. Kids help by feeding animals and harvesting crops.

The whole family helps harvest rice.

Floating Markets

People travel on canals in boats called sampans. Farmers sell rice, fish, coconuts, chickens, and vegetables from their boats. Shoppers hop from boat to boat looking for items to buy.

17

At street-side cafes, vendors sell bowls of rice with many choices of toppings. Diners grab tasty morsels with chopsticks (thin wooden sticks).

A woman separates rice grains from their stalks.

Rice

Rice, rice, everywhere rice! Vietnamese people work so hard to grow rice because they eat it at almost every meal.

Cooks make rice noodles to plop into soups. Slurp! Rice is even made into wine.

Lunch is the biggest meal of the day. A bowl of steaming rice is always on the table. Diners might add a tasty fish sauce and cooked vegetables to the meal. Fish, pork, beef, or bean curd (tofu) might be tasty side dishes.

Huge heaps of rice noodles are for sale at open-air markets.

Vietnam's flag flies on top of the Army Museum in Hanoi (left). Visitors can view weapons and war artifacts from Vietnam's many battles. This statue shows North Vietnamese leader Ho Chi Minh (below). The city of Saigon was renamed Ho Chi Minh City for this important leader in 1975.

History

Vietnam used to be two countries. The northern half was called North Vietnam. Can you guess what

the southern half was named? South Vietnam! Each half wanted to rule the other.

A war between the two countries lasted from the 1950s to the 1970s. In 1976 North Vietnam won, and Vietnam became one country again.

Vietnam's Flag

In 1955 the Vietnamese chose a flag for their country. The red background stands for **revolution.** The star symbolizes **Communism,** Vietnam's system of government.

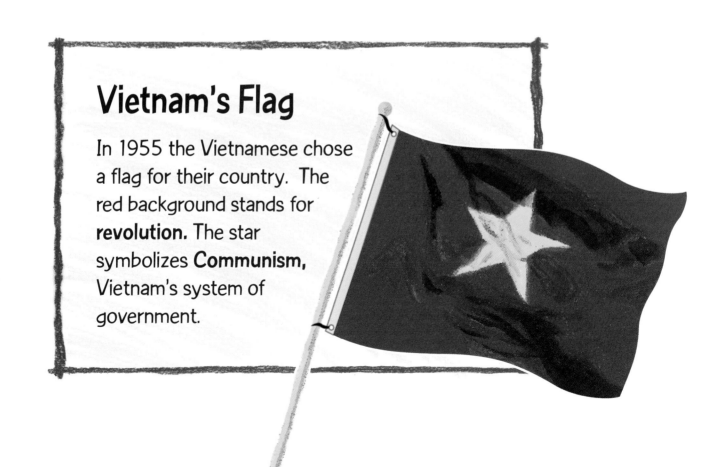

At Home

In Vietnam people choose all sorts of places to live. In the northern countryside, some people like cozy stone houses. In the south, many pick airy wooden homes. City dwellers may squeeze into apartments.

As many as 40 Montagnard family members may call this longhouse home.

Houses on stilts (facing page) *keep families dry during flood season. Early Chinese settlers left their mark on Vietnam with many fancy temples* (right).

A house near a river might perch on stilts! The tall poles keep the homes safe from floods when it rains. And when the weather is dry, people and animals can enjoy the shade under the house.

A traditional Vietnamese art form is called lacquerware. To make this dragon, Vietnamese artists glued shapes onto wood and covered it with a shiny, clear paint.

Made by Hand

Some Vietnamese kids help their parents make crafts. People create and decorate beautiful wooden boxes and furniture. Others weave silk (a rich fabric) or make boats, baskets, or hats. Experts carve wooden blocks that they use to print colorful fabric and pictures. Artists skillfully shape clay into cups, plates, or animal shapes. These items are sold at open-air markets.

Artists show off some wood-block prints (above).

Silk's Story

Silk is made from the cocoons of silkworms, a kind of caterpillar. Workers unwind the tiny cocoons and use the strands to weave silk.

25

Clothes

Most people in
Vietnam wear
practical cotton
shirts and pants. A
non la (a cone-shaped
hat) might top the

City girls (above) dress up for a ride through town. Non las are popular with workers in the country (left).

outfit. The hats keep off both hot sun and pouring rain. On special occasions, people put on fancy outfits. Men wear a loose top and pants. Women put on a long top with the sides slit to the waist and long pants.

Two girls bike to their final exams wearing traditional Vietnamese clothing.

School

At age six, Vietnamese kids begin school. There is no such thing as a summer vacation. Kids go to school six days a week, all year long. But some kids take time off to help their parents work on the family farm.

Kids of all ages attend this country schoolhouse.

To keep class size down, some kids attend school in the morning, and others go to class in the afternoon.

Vietnamese kids do not get report cards. Instead, teachers send home notes that tell parents how their child is doing in school.

Buddhist temples often display statues of Buddha.

Faith

Vietnamese people might follow one of many faiths. About half of the people are Buddhists. They believe in a cycle of life and rebirth. Some Vietnamese people are Taoists, who try to live in harmony with nature. They believe in many gods, such as the Jade Emperor who rules heaven. Lots of Vietnamese people combine belief systems.

Pagodas (above) *are holy places for Buddhists to go and pray. Many houses have altars* (right) *for loved ones who have died.*

People celebrate Tet Nguyen Dan in many ways (left). Cooks prepare banh chung (below).

Celebrate!

The biggest holiday in Vietnam is Tet Nguyen Dan, New Year's Day. Everyone is on their best behavior. Folks wear new clothes. People who had fights make up, and others pay back loans.

Fireworks and parades make the holiday fun. People visit friends and eat treats such as fried watermelon seeds, *banh chung,* and pickled vegetables. Banh chung is a squishy rice cake filled with bean paste and pork.

Kids pick out strings of fireworks to set off on Tet Nguyen Dan.

The Moon Festival

The Moon Festival celebrates the autumn harvest. Boys and girls use rice paper to make lanterns shaped like fish or stars and hang them on long, bamboo poles. After dark the youngsters carry the lit lanterns in a parade.

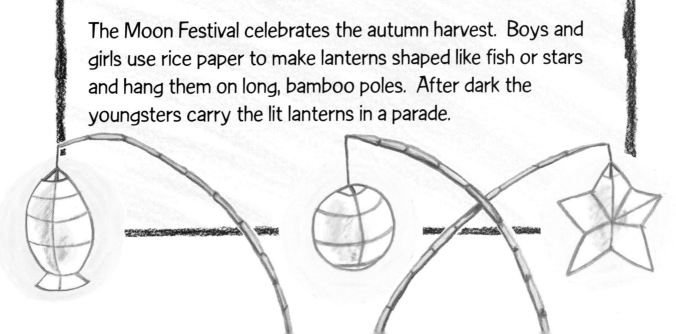

A skilled musician plays a zither that has one string. Music is important to the Vietnamese.

Music

Some Vietnamese musicians play drums, gongs, and cymbals. Others pipe on flutes. A dried gourd, a curved stick, and a long copper wire make an instrument called a *dan bau*. The *dan tam* is like a guitar with three strings.

During one spring festival, boys sing a verse of a song they make up on the spot!

Some religious ceremonies include music.

Then girls sing back different words. But for most of the year, many young folks listen to pop music.

This musical instrument, called a to rung, is a xylophone made out of stones!

Speak Vietnamese

Speaking Vietnamese is like singing a song! There are high and low tones, changing tones, and flat tones. A word can have one of many different meanings, depending

What a Character!

In the past, Vietnamese was written using **characters** to represent words. These days people use letters like the ones used in this book. Characters are still used for decoration *(left)*.

on the tone. If you say the word *ma* in a high tone, you mean "mother." In a low tone, *ma* means "rice plant." With a flat tone, *ma* is the word for "ghost." If you are not careful, you might say, "Is that your ghost?" instead of, "Is that your mother?"

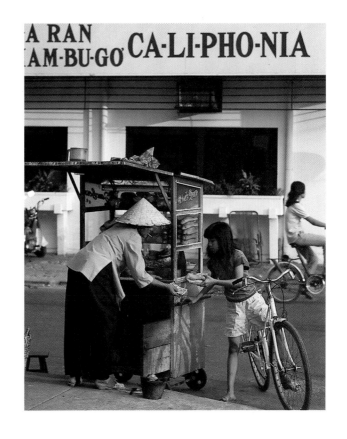

Artists use characters to decorate (top). *But most Vietnamese write using English-style letters* (right).

Poems and Stories

Poetry is BIG in Vietnam. Not only is it very popular, but poems can be hundreds of verses long.

Vietnamese people love folktales, too. Some tell about how the world came to be the way it is. One story, called *The Legend of 100 Sons,* is so popular that there is a festival to celebrate it!

The Legend of 100 Sons

The mountain spirit, Au Co, married a water dragon named Lac Long. The couple had 100 sons who hatched from 100 eggs. Lac Long wanted to live by the sea. But Au Co wanted to live in the mountains. Half of the children went with their father. The other 50 lived in the mountains with their mother. According to legend, the sons who went to the sea became the Vietnamese people.

Time for Fun

Kids love ice-cream parlors and hanging out with friends. In most villages, community centers have televisions and pool tables.

These women do morning exercises to start the day on the right (or left!) foot.

Many Vietnamese youngsters play soccer, volleyball, or tennis. Some Vietnamese take up **martial arts.** On hot days, kids cool off with a dip in a canal, in the ocean, or in a river.

A trip to the beach is the perfect way to pass a sunny day.

Vietnamese teens shoot a game of pool at the local community center.

Puppets glide across the water, acting out Vietnamese stories.

Water Puppets

Vietnamese kids love to watch water
puppetry. A pond is the stage! Grown-ups
and kids sit on the shore of a pond or stream.
Behind a bamboo screen, puppeteers stand
in water up to their knees. The puppeteers
use underwater rods to make the brightly
painted wooden puppets glide over the

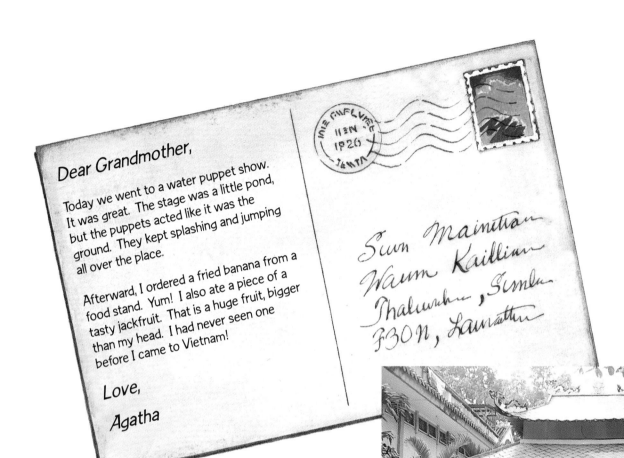

Dear Grandmother,

Today we went to a water puppet show. It was great. The stage was a little pond, but the puppets acted like it was the ground. They kept splashing and jumping all over the place.

Afterward, I ordered a fried banana from a food stand. Yum! I also ate a piece of a tasty jackfruit. That is a huge fruit, bigger than my head. I had never seen one before I came to Vietnam!

Love,

Agatha

Sun Mainitian
Waum Kaillian
Thalunhu , Simlu
730 N, Lamattin

water. The puppets look like clowns, musicians, heroes, princes, and princesses.

Puppeteers hide behind this beautiful building's bamboo screen. The puppets seem to move on their own.

43

The Vietnamese bring cherry and apricot blossoms into their houses during Tet Nguyen Dan to help bring good luck.

New Words to Learn

bargain: A talk between a buyer and seller about the cost of an item. Bargaining ends when both sides agree on a price.

canal: A waterway made by humans to link rivers to one another.

character: A symbol that stands for a whole word or a word sound. In past times, Vietnamese was always written using characters.

communism: A system of government in which the state owns and runs all or most businesses.

continent: Any one of seven large areas of land. A few of the continents are Africa, Asia, and North America.

delta: A triangle of land formed where a river enters an ocean.

ethnic group: A group of people with many things in common, such as language, religion, and customs.

ethnic Vietnamese: A person with ancestors from Vietnam's largest ethnic group.

map: A drawing or chart of all or part of the earth or sky.

martial art: One of several ways of fighting and of protecting oneself. Martial arts include judo, kendo, aikido, and karate.

monsoon: A strong wind that brings rain to Vietnam and its neighboring countries.

mountain range: A series, or group, of mountains—the parts of the earth's surface that rise high into the sky.

revolution: When the people of a country throw out their ruler and make a new government for themselves.

rice paddy: A wet field on which farmers grow rice.

tropical rain forest: A thick, green forest that gets lots of rain every year.

typhoon: A big storm with strong winds and heavy rain.

New Words to Say

Annamite	ahn-NAHM-myte
Au Co	OW KAH
banh chung	BAHN CHIHNG
Buddhist	BOO-dihst
cyclo	SY-cloh
dan bau	YAHNG BOW
dan tam	YAHNG TAHM
Hanoi	hah-NOY
Ho Chi Minh	HOH CHEE MIHN
Lac Long	LOHK LAHNG
Mekong	MAY-kahng
monsoon	mahn-SOON
Montagnard	moh^n-tahn-YAHRD
My Nuong	MY NOO-uhn
non la	NAHN LAH
Taoist	DOW-ihst
Tet Nguyen Dan	TEHT ^{n}WEEN DAHN
typhoon	ty-FOON
Vietnam	vee-EHT-nahm

More Books to Read

Allard, Denise. *Postcards from Vietnam.* Austin, TX: Raintree/Steck-Vaughn, 1997.

Jacobsen, Karen. *A New True Book: Vietnam.* Chicago: Children's Press, Inc., 1992.

Lee, Jeanne M. *Toad Is the Uncle of Heaven: A Vietnamese Folk Tale.* New York: Henry Holt, 1989.

Lorbiecki, Marybeth. *Children of Vietnam.* Minneapolis: Carolrhoda Books, Inc., 1997.

Scoones, Simon. *A Family from Vietnam.* Austin, TX: Raintree/Steck-Vaughn, 1998.

Shephard, Aaron. *The Crystal Heart : A Vietnamese Legend.* New York: Atheneum, 1998.

New Words to Find